Am I special?

Stephen Hogue
illustrated by Chris Swink

Artwork by: Chris Swink

Revised and reprinted - 2018

Published by EA Books Publishing a division of
Living Parables of Central Florida Inc, a 501c3
EABooksPublishing.com

DEDICATION

I dedicate this book to my beautiful wife, Sandra, who has been so patient and helpful in seeing my dreams become a reality. I also dedicate it to my ten amazing, adopted kids, whose adoption stories inspired me to write this book.

Josie lived with her mom and dad and her Grandma. One day Josie's Grandma was cleaning out the attic. She found some old pictures of Josie's Grandpa before they were married.

"Why is Grandpa dressed like that, Grandma?"
"He was a soldier Josie", exclaimed her Grandma in a tender voice.
"What's a soldier?", asked Josie. Her Grandma replied, "A soldier is someone who fights for his or her country."

"He was a very special man", said Grandma. "I wish I had known him", replied Josie. Her Grandma explained that he died when she was just a baby. Josie asked, "What is special?" Her Grandma answered, "Special means something or someone is very important to you."

Josie walked away wondering to herself... "Am I special?"

Next, she went into the garage where her Dad was working.

"Whatcha doing, Daddy?"

He said, "I'm working on this old car."
Josie asked, "Why Daddy?"

"Well honey", her Dad said, "this is a very special car. This car has been in our family since my Grandfather had it."

"I want to fix it up like it was when he had it." Josie asked, "Why is it special?" Dad said, "Because it has been in our family for many years and it reminds me of my Grandfather, your great Grandfather. I remember riding with my Grandfather in this car when I was a little boy. I have some very fond memories about this special car. It is very important to me."

Josie walked out of the garage wondering, "Am I important?"

Later, Josie walked into the kitchen and her mom was washing dishes.

Josie asked, "Mommy, why don't we use the nice dishes that you keep in the china cabinet?"

"Well sweetie, those are for special occasions, like holidays or when we have guests at our house for dinner."

"Why are those dishes so special?", asked Josie.

"Well, because they were a very valuable wedding gift your daddy and I received."

"What does valuable mean?" asked Josie.

"Valuable means they are worth a lot."

As Josie walked away she
wondered to herself...
"Am I valuable?"

Josie walked into the living room where there was a cabinet where her mom kept all their family photo albums. Josie found the one that had her baby pictures. Josie's story is a little different than most kids.

She was adopted. Her parents picked her up from the hospital when she was just a week old. They had to go to court and see a judge to complete the adoption.

She didn't remember, but she could look at all the pictures and see what happened. She thought about how she wasn't like many of her friends. Their moms had them in their tummies. But not Josie. Josie's birth mother couldn't take care of her. Because she loved her so much, she decided to put her up for adoption. Josie started to cry.

"I'm not so special." she thought.
"If I was special my mom would not have given me away."

Her mom heard her crying and went to her room and asked,
"What's wrong Josie?"

"I guess I'm not very special. I'm not like all the other kids. I'm adopted."

Josie's mom sat down on the floor and began to tell her the whole story.

"Josie, when Daddy and I were first married, the doctors told us that we would not be able to have children.

I was very sad."

"Daddy and I prayed for God to give us the right baby at the right time. One day, we received a call about a baby girl who needed a family. We drove for two hours to the hospital you were born in. When we first saw you, we just cried."

"We didn't cry because we were sad. We cried because we were so happy. We chose you, Josie. God gave us YOU to adopt and that gave us great joy."

"Out of all the kids that were able to be adopted, we chose you! That makes you so special!"

Josie's frown began to turn into a smile.

"Josie, you are a gift! Don't ever feel bad that you are adopted. We prayed for you to come to us and God answered that prayer by giving us the most special little girl in the whole world."

Josie and her mom just hugged for a long time. "Thanks for choosing me mommy." said Josie.

"Now I know that I am special, important and valuable."

You made all the delicate, inner parts of my body and knit me together in my mother's womb. Thank you for making me so wonderfully complex! Your workmanship is marvelous—how well I know it.

Psalms 139:13-14 NLT

Adoption has many faces. It can be **domestic** (within the United States, through a private adoption agency or law firm), it can be **international** (overseas), or it can be adoption through the **foster care** system. The process to adopt and the price to adopt varies, based on agency, country, whether it's a single adoption or siblings, etc. Domestic and international adoptions can cost thousands of dollars. However, adoption through foster care is usually minimal to no cost at all.

Each year in the US, there are approximately 50,000 domestic adoptions. Ironically, there are also about 50,000 children adopted from foster care every year. Kids and teens enter foster care because of abuse, neglect and/or abandonment. There are approximately 100,000 children in the foster care system waitng to be adopted.

For more information about domestic or international adoption, you can search online for trusted agencies. For information about foster care adoption, contact your local child welfare agency and read about the ones who are available for adoption, by going to www.adoptuskids.org.

James 1:27 says that pure and undefiled religion is to care for orphans and widows in their time of need and to remain unspotted by the world.

To learn more about how your church can be involved in fulfilling James 1:27 within the foster care system, contact www.hoguecrew.org

HOGUE MINISTRIES
www.hoguecrew.org

Follow us on Social Media:
 Hogue Crew

To support Hogue Ministries please visit:
hoguecrew.org/give
or
Text "Give" and dollar amount to
(386) 961 4747